AF735513

Patrick Kerr and Helen Waller are both barristers at 12 King's Bench Walk, one of the leading sets of chambers specialising in personal injury litigation. Both authors are road cyclists and specialise in claims involving cycling.

Patrick is a leading junior ranked by both Chambers & Partners and the Legal 500. He is frequently instructed in claims involving professional cyclists, including those who have suffered career-ending injuries.

Helen is regularly instructed by both claimants and defendants as both sole and junior counsel in cycling claims involving serious, catastrophic or fatal injuries. She is much sought after as a trainer in cycling law.

A Practical Guide to Injury Claims involving Cyclists

A Practical Guide to Injury Claims involving Cyclists

Patrick Kerr
Barrister,
12 Kings Bench Walk

Helen Waller
Barrister,
12 Kings Bench Walk

Law Brief Publishing

Published 2022 by Law Brief Publishing, an imprint of Law Brief Publishing Ltd
30 The Parks
Minehead
Somerset
TA24 8BT

www.lawbriefpublishing.com

Paperback: 978-1-914608-04-9

CONTENTS

Chapter One	Introduction	1
Chapter Two	Cyclists as Road Users	5
Chapter Three	Sportives, Coached Cycling and Group Rides	19
Chapter Four	Professional Cycling	33
Chapter Five	Highways Cases	41
Chapter Six	Contributory Negligence	49
Chapter Seven	Cycle Helmets	55

CHAPTER ONE

INTRODUCTION

Cycling continues to grow in popularity, led by an increase in female riders, according to the statistics released by Sport England. The annual Sport England Active Lives survey, published in October 2019 (before the pandemic), showed that approximately 100,000 more people were cycling for leisure and sport than in the previous year. That alone is reason enough to produce a book concerning the civil law surrounding cycling. Additionally, however, the latest edition of the Highway Code, which came out only weeks ago, has been viewed by many as significantly shifting the emphasis of the law and guidance surrounding cycling. The revised and updated Code has caused some consternation, at least within some news and social media outlets. On 15 February 2022, the Daily Express described the "fury" surrounding rules that are designed to protect vulnerable road users, reporting a "demand that cyclists should be obliged to take a 'driving test'". A day later, the Daily Mail described the revised Code as "controversial", suggesting its implementation should be delayed so as to avoid a "spike in road rage incidents" given the "adverse impact on the country's motorists". The key complaint, it appears, is that "someone driving will have more responsibly to watch out for people cycling, walking or riding a horse." Neither article analyses why less responsibility to watch out for more vulnerable road uses could be considered a good thing; or why the desire to make drivers more vigilant is too onerous.

In any event, it is hoped this book will help explain why the "new" rules are perhaps less novel or controversial than some commentators appear to be believe; and what impact they are likely to have on civil litigation involving cycling. The book is not, however, merely a recitation of the Highway Code. It also looks to analyse the current case law and statutory obligations relating to every aspect of cycling, from a road user's duty of care and contributory negligence to injuries in the professional peloton. The aim is to give the reader a swift but comprehensive overview of the law as it stands, and some suggestions as to how it may evolve in the near future.

The book does not have a chapter specifically dealing with e-bikes and e-scooters as proper analysis of these forms of transport would likely amount to a volume in itself, not least because they have their own rules and regulations separate to fully self-propelled bicycles. For instance, there is an age restriction to electric bikes (you need to be 14 years or older to ride one); there is obligatory information that must be displayed (the power output or the manufacturer of the motor / the battery's voltage or the bike's maximum speed); and the e-bike must be restricted in maximum power output and must cut out at a certain speed (250 watts and 15.5mph respectively). However, it is worth noting that if an e-bike does conform to these strictures, it is classed as an "electrically assisted pedal cycle" (EAPC) and treated as a normal pedal bike and therefore can be ridden on cycle paths and anywhere else pedal bikes are allowed. If they do not conform, they are classed as motorcycles or mopeds and need to be registered and taxed – and require a driving licence and a crash helmet in order to be ridden.

For the same reason, there is no chapter on mobility scooters or powered wheelchairs, both of which have their own set of rules depending on type: class 2 – which cannot be used on the road and are limited to 4mph – and class 3, which can be used on the road and are limited to 8mph. They are treated very differently to pedal bicycles, with all types of mobility scooter and powered wheelchair being legally allowed on footpaths and pedestrian areas[1], but being banned from cycle paths marked 'cycle only'.

---

[1] Bicycles are statutorily banned from doing so: s. 72 of the Highways Act 1835 (for an offence in England and Wales) and s. 129 of the Roads (Scotland) Act 1984.

The law surrounding the introduction of semi-autonomous vehicles on to our roads, on the other hand, would not amount to more than a few paragraphs, let alone a chapter or book, so again, this is not subject to much analysis in (this edition?) of the book. Obviously, this is an area of law which will require considerable legislation in due course, but at present, there is little to say other than we have to wait and see.

These topics aside, it is hoped that this book is a useful, practical guide to an area of litigation which is increasing in volume and significance. As published by HM Government on 30 September 2021, cycling fatalities have increased by 5% from 2004 to 2020; serious injuries have rocketed by 26%; and pedal cycle traffic has grown by 96%. Between 2015 and 2020, an average of 2 pedal cyclists are killed and 83 seriously injured per week[2]. Most commonly, these deaths and serious injuries involve another vehicle, overwhelmingly either a car or a heavy goods vehicle[3], so it is fair to say, the law surrounding the world of cycling is worth knowing.

Insofar as it is ever appropriate to dedicate a slim volume like this to a person, we would like to dedicate it to our friend and colleague, Richard Viney, who sadly lost his life in a cycling accident in August 2021. A brilliant barrister and experienced cyclist, his loss is, and will always be, keenly felt by many of us. May he ride in peace.

---

[2] https://www.gov.uk/government/statistics/reported-road-casualties-great-britain-pedal-cyclist-factsheet-2020/reported-road-casualties-in-great-britain-pedal-cycle-factsheet-2020

[3] It should be emphasised, however, that the government factsheet rightly points out that factors contributing to a collision or accident are largely subjective as they reflect the opinion of the reporting police officer. To quote the factsheet: *"They are assigned quickly at the occurrence of the collision and often without extensive investigations and so should be interpreted with caution. They are likely to be affected in part by preconceptions police officers have of certain vehicle groups."*

The content of this book is believed to be accurate and up-to-date based on the law as it was on 15th March 2022.

CHAPTER TWO

CYCLISTS AS ROAD USERS

The Highway Code

As road users, cyclists are subject to the Highway Code just like pedestrians and other vehicular traffic. The Code itself is of mixed status. Many of its rules are legal requirements. If you break those rules, you are committing a legal offence. These rules are identified by the use of "MUST/MUST NOT". However, most of the rules in the Highway Code are advisory rather than mandatory. A failure to comply with these rules will not of itself mean that a road user has committed an offence or been negligent, but the failure can be used as evidence of negligence (see section 38(7) of The Road Traffic Act 1988).

January 2022 saw the introduction of a new Highway Code, bringing in a "hierarchy of road users" and a number of updates to the rules in respect of cyclists. The hierarchy emphasises a point already well known to lawyers dealing with road traffic cases and arguments of contributory negligence: "*those in charge of vehicles that can cause the greatest harm in the event of a collision bear the greatest responsibility to take care and reduce the danger they pose to others*"[4]. That reflects the "causative potency" aspect of contributory negligence analyses. The expounding of this hierarchy in the Code doesn't actually change the liability landscape amongst road users, therefore. What it does do, though, is make the position very clear to lay persons.

[4] Highway Code, Rule H1.

There are a number of other updates in the new Highway Code that are of interest to cyclists and, indeed, to others sharing the road with cyclists. Here it is worth noting that "road" in this context generally includes footpaths, bridleways and cycle tracks.

An important inclusion in the new Code is that drivers and motorcyclists "*should not cut across cyclists, horse riders or horse drawn vehicles going ahead when you are turning into or out of a junction or changing direction or lane*". Further, motorists should "*not turn at a junction if to do so would cause the cyclist, horse rider or horse drawn vehicle going straight ahead to stop or swerve*".[5] See also **Rule 76**, which sets out that when going straight ahead at a junction cyclists have priority over traffic waiting to turn into or out of a side road.

At the time of writing, it is too soon to know whether this inclusion will materially change liability analyses, but the wording of the rule certainly does put greater responsibility on the motorist than under the previous rules. It is an unfortunately common scenario to have a collision occur where a motorist has turned left off a main road into a side road, across the path of a cyclist travelling down the main road. Each case is of course fact dependent, but to date it has often been the case that an injured cyclist in that scenario would be found to have been contributorily negligent to some degree, typically for failing to anticipate that the motorist might turn and act accordingly. The new rule gives the cyclist right of way to carry on along the main road, putting the onus on the motorist to check and wait until the cyclist is clear. This is undoubtedly good news for cyclists.

The core rules in the Highway Code that are relevant to cyclists are found in rules 59 to 71. Most of these are advisory, rather than mandatory. A few are worth highlighting.

---

[5] Rule H3.

The mandatory **Rule 60** states that at night "*your cycle MUST have white front and red rear lights lit. It MUST also be fitted with a red rear reflector (and amber pedal reflectors, if manufactured after 1/10/85)*". This rule comes from The Road Vehicles Lighting Regulations 1989.

When dealing with a cycling accident case that occurred at night, checking what lights and reflectors the bike had (and whether the lights were on) will be important, therefore. Despite the wording of the rule, lights will be more important than reflectors when considering any negligence of the cyclist and how visible the bicycle was. Interestingly, most road bikes with clipless pedals won't have any reflectors at all. However, most road cycling shoes will have a reflective portion on the heel and many saddle bags also have a reflective strip or similar. When considering civil liability in this context it is suggested that it is the overall visibility of the cyclist that should be important. A lack of pedal reflectors is unlikely to be causally material except in most particular circumstances.

Rule 66 deals with group riding. It states "*You can ride two abreast and it can be safer to do so, particularly in larger groups or when accompanying children or less experienced riders*". The wording of this is important. It is a change from the previous Highway Code which was more prescriptive, stating "*never ride more than two abreast, and ride in single file on narrow or busy roads when riding around bends*". The new rule, therefore, allows the cyclist(s) to decide what is appropriate in the particular context. This will of course be fodder for many an argument at trial about whether it was reasonable to be riding two abreast on a particular road.

Riding two-by-two is generally the favoured approach of groups of cyclists, especially those on road bikes out for training rides. When in tight formation, this is known as a "chain-gang". Such a formation typically allows cyclists to ride faster and more efficiently. In theory, it should also be a safer way to ride as a group on the roads than being spread out in single file as it means that motorists only have one, concentrated group to overtake, rather than a string of individual cyclists. Nevertheless, chain-gangs often attract a lot of ire from motorists.

Cyclists within chain-gangs owe a duty of care to one another, as well as to other road users. Those from the second row backwards are reliant on the cyclists in front identifying hazards or obstacles in good time and indicating those to the rest of the group accordingly. Indeed, cyclist claimants have had significant reductions applied for contributory negligence for cycling at an unsafe distance from the cyclist in front (see, for example, *Thomas v Warwickshire CC* [2011] EWHC 772 (QB)). Although the authors have not been able to find any reported caselaw on the point, in theory a cyclist in a chain-gang could bring a claim in negligence against another cyclist in that chain-gang if, for example, the cyclist out front failed to warn about an upcoming pothole, which the following cyclist then hit and came off.

In *Nicol v Kupinski* [2017] 10 WLUK 721, a lorry driver was found liable for causing a collision between two cyclists in a chain-gang, despite the lorry not making contact with either cyclist. The claimant was cycling in a chain-gang of four when the group went to pass a lorry parked with its hazard lights on in the nearside of two lanes on a two-lane carriageway. As the group went to pass the lorry, the lorry suddenly went to move off. This prompted the first cyclist into taking immediate evasive action, braking sharply and veering. The claimant, cycling behind, also braked sharply but was unable to take evasive action and so collided with the first cyclist's rear. The claimant brought a claim against the lorry driver, who in response submitted that the court should make a finding of contributory negligence which should be assessed at 75% where the claimant had breached the Highway Code by cycling too close to the cyclist in front of her. The court found in favour of the claimant, holding that the lorry driver had failed to take reasonable care for the safety of other road users.

The court further declined to find any contributory negligence, holding that such a finding was not supported.

Rule 69 is concise and mandatory: "*You MUST obey all traffic signs and traffic light signals*". Many cyclists do indeed obey all signs and signals. Many do not. Cycling through a red light is undeniably going to be a breach of a cyclist's duty of care to other road users and, therefore, prima facie negligent. Yet the key question for a court when considering an accident involving that cyclist is going to be one of causation. Did jumping the light actually cause the accident? The answer will of course be fact specific.

Although one might think that jumping a red light would support a conclusion that this is a cyclist who is reckless, it is cautiously suggested that that is not necessarily always the case. It is possible to argue that jumping a light could, in fact (if not in law) have been the safer option in some contexts. For example, to escape an aggressive motorist or to get clear of very heavy traffic. It is important to remember that in the context of a cyclist accident claim, the question is what was reasonable <u>in the particular circumstances</u>, which can be far more nuanced than simply whether the various road users obeyed the rules.

Rules 72 deals with road positioning. This can be an important area of analysis in a cycling accident case, sometimes requiring expert accident reconstruction evidence looking at both visibility and causation. The new Highway Code states that there are two basic road positions: the centre of the lane, making yourself clearly visible, or towards the nearside kerb on busier roads, still keeping at least 0.5m from the kerb. This is a new addition to the Highway Code and, it is suggested, a welcome one. It is clear that cyclists aren't obliged to stick to the left of their lane, and riding in the centre of the lane may be the best and most reasonable option in many circumstances.

Although filtering has always been a bit of a grey area, with the Highway Code never expressly condoning or condemning it, the new Highway Code for 2022 suggests that filtering on a bike past slow or stationary traffic is now given more protection. **Rule 67** expressly acknowledges filtering on the left, stating, "*when cycling on the road, only pass to the left of large vehicles when they are stationary or slow moving and you should proceed with caution as the driver may not be able to see you*". Then **Rule 163**, nominally addressing overtaking, acknowledges filtering on both the left and right by cyclists: "*Cyclists may pass slower moving or stationary traffic on their right or left and should proceed with caution as the driver may not be able to see you*". The new wording of **Rules 160** and **211** is such that drivers must give way to cyclists when changing direction or lane, and that drivers must not turn at a junction if to do so would cause a cyclist going straight ahead to stop or swerve. That appears to lend filtering cyclists a little more protection. Filtering cyclists are of course still under the same duty to take reasonable care for other road users, but it will be interesting to see if these additions to the Highway Code have any impact on how the courts view the practice.

Duty of Care

> "*An underlying principle of the law of the highway is that all those lawfully using the highway … must show mutual respect and forbearance*"
>
> – per Lord du Parcq, *Searle v Wallbank* [1947] AC 341 at 361

Cyclists owe a duty to all other road users to cycle with reasonable care. The rules and guidance contained in the Highway Code are a good yardstick against which to measure the reasonableness of a cyclist's behaviour. Nonetheless, it is worth noting that a breach of the Highway Code is not of itself determinative of negligence, albeit it is likely to carry significant weight. Cyclists also owe a duty of care to themselves to take reasonable care for their own safety whilst cycling. This can be relevant when evaluating a cyclist's behaviour in the context of allegations of contributory negligence (see, for example, *Kotula v EDF Energy Networks (EPN) Plc* [2010] WLUK 234, which is addressed in the chapter on contributory negligence).

"Reasonable care" means the care which an ordinarily skilful cyclist would have exercised in all the circumstances. It includes all the aspects one would expect of any road user, such as avoiding excessive speed, keeping a good look out, observing traffic rules and signals, etc. That duty of reasonable care is owed to all other road users as well as persons and their property on land adjacent to the highway. What is reasonable will depend on the road user and on the circumstances.

An interesting point to note with respect to cyclists' duty of care is that they are not subjected to speed limits like motorised road users are. Rather, what is important is what is reasonably safe in the circumstances. **Rule 124** of the Highway Code includes a table that sets out the speed limits for various types of vehicle on various categories of road. The table does not include bicycles. As such, cyclists who exceed the national speed limit for a road may not be prosecuted for a speeding offence but they can, however, be prosecuted for "cycling furiously" or "wanton and furious cycling."

The new hierarchy of road users set out in the Highway Code makes it clear that cyclists have a responsibility to reduce danger to pedestrians. In recent years there have been numerous newspaper headlines reporting collisions between cyclists and pedestrians. As cycling grows as a mode of transport in cities in particular, such collisions are likely to become more frequent.

An often overlooked aspect of the cyclist's duty of care is that to keep his or her bicycle in good working order. When dealing with a case of a collision involving a cyclist, it is worth enquiring when the bike was purchased, when it was last serviced, if the tyres were properly inflated, when the brakes were last checked or replaced and so on. Indeed, the requirement for brakes on pedal bikes and the need for them to be in efficient working order is set out in The Pedal Cycles Regulations 1983. Tyres pressures and the state of a bicycle's brakes can impact its stopping distance and may be relevant to both breach and causation. Even static factors such as a bicycle's wheel size can be relevant as this can have an effect on the cyclist's control over his or her steering.

In cycling accident cases though it's not just the duty of care of the cyclist and other road users that might be relevant. For example, there may be an occupiers' liability angle where an accident has occurred because of the infrastructure.

In the Scottish case of *Fairley v Edinburgh Trams Ltd* [2019] CSOH 50, two cyclists were awarded damages for injuries that they sustained while cycling across tram tracks in Edinburgh. They successfully proved that the infrastructure at each accident location was hazardous since it required cyclists to cross the tram tracks at too shallow an angle. The risk of crossing tram tracks at too shallow an angle was held to be one that was not obvious, but which was known or reasonably foreseeable to the local roads authority.

A similar case, *Liddle v Bristol City Council* [2018] EWH C 3673 (QB), failed where it was held that the local authority had taken reasonable steps to see that cyclists were reasonably safe. The claim was made following the tragic death of a cyclist who had fallen off Prince's Harbour Wharf in Bristol after his rear wheel got stuck in a tram rail on the wharf. There was signage on the wharf warning of tracks that were dangerous to cyclists. However, it was held that these were not sufficient to enable a reasonable cyclist to realise that he or she was forbidden from going beyond a certain point. Nevertheless, the signage was sufficient warning of the danger and there was an alternative cycle path available to be taken. The court held that the defendant had taken reasonable steps to see that lawful visitors were reasonably safe.

Another interesting cycling case brought under the Occupiers' Liability Act 1957 is *Hood v Forestry Commission* [2017] 3 WLUK 189. That case involved a claimant who was injured whilst cycling along a mountain-bike trail in Cumbria. He alleged that a boardwalk, over which he had to cycle, was slippery and unsafe and that this had caused his bike to slip, resulting in him falling and fracturing his leg. The claim failed. It was held that the claimant was an experienced rider who knew he was riding in wet conditions on a difficult trail. The court concluded that slipping was not a hazard that had to be guarded against at all costs, and that the defendant had discharged its duty in grooving and cross-hatching the boardwalk.

Cycle Lanes

Rules 61 and **62** of the Highway Code deal with cycle lanes and tracks. The Code is clear that although these are provided for reasons of safety, cyclists are not obliged to use them. Rather, cyclists may exercise their judgement, based on their experience, skills and the situation at the time, to decide whether or not to use the cycle lane or track. The lack of an obligation on cyclists to use cycle lanes or tracks is re-stated in **Rule 140**.

Rule 140 of the Code forms part of the general rules, techniques and advice for all drivers and riders. It states that drivers "*MUST NOT drive or park in a cycle lane marked by a solid white line during its times operation*". Further, "*Do not drive or park in a cycle lane marked by a broken white line unless it is unavoidable*". Importantly, it goes on to advise that "*You should give way to any cyclists in a cycle lane, including when they are approaching from behind you,*" and "*You should give way to cyclists approaching or using the cycle track when you are turning into or out of a junction.*"

Cycle lanes are those marked by a solid or broken white line (see The Traffic Signs Regulations and General Directions 2002, Section 4) that run along the carriageway. Cycle tracks are routes that are physically protected or located away from motor traffic (see also, the Cycle Tracks Act 1984). Some cycle tracks are shared with pedestrians and on such routes cyclists are advised to always take care when passing pedestrians, leaving plenty of room, and being prepared to slow down and stop if necessary.

Sometimes it will be the cycle lane / track itself that is alleged to constitute the danger. For example, where a cycle lane has raised white lines either side – a potential hazard for narrow wheels – or where the layout of the cycle lane exposes cyclists to a danger from traffic. The requirements for the design of cycle lanes and tracks is generally found in Local Transport Notes, known as LTNs. For example, the "Cycle Infrastructure Design" LTN of July 2020 from the Department for Transport is the updated national guidance for highway authorities and designers, produced with the aim of helping cycling become a form of mass transit. When considering cycling infrastructure design, it is important to identify and read closely the relevant LTN(s) in force at the time. Sustrans, an organisation that is the custodian of the National Cycle Network, is another valuable resource of cycling infrastructure guidance. In considering cycling infrastructure and whether it itself presents a danger, it is worth thinking about the road layout, highway structures and bridges, drainage systems and road lighting, amongst other matters.

The Scottish case of *Wallace v Roache* [20 21] SAC (Civ) 23 is a case involving a cycle path and an interesting example of how, even despite the vastly greater causative potency of a car as opposed to a bike, the car driver could be found to be at no or, alternatively, little (15%) fault. In *Wallace*, a cyclist had been injured in a collision at an intersection of a national cycle path and an access road. The access road had priority over the cycle path at the intersection. There were prominent 'Give Way' signs in both directions for cyclists on approach. As the cyclist approached the intersection, he was riding at around 20mph, which is quite a considerable speed on a bike. He was in the middle of the cycle path. He did not brake or reduce his speed on approach and he ignored the give way sign. The defendant had been driving down the access road at a speed of no more than 15mph. He had seen the cycle path warning sign and was keeping a lookout. He was able to see the cycle path to his right, but he wanted to clear a hedge running parallel to the cycle path in order to get a line of sight to his left. As he moved forward to do so, he was struck by the claimant's bicycle. The Sheriff found that that fundamental cause of the accident was the negligent and irresponsible action of the cyclist in failing to comply with the give way sign. In considering the cycle track itself, at paragraph 17 of the judgment, the Sheriff stated that, "*There is no substance to the suggestion by the pursuer that he was less culpable or blameworthy because he was on a leisure path designed to separate him from motor traffic and was only a danger to himself*". The driver was found to have been aware of the risk of there being a cyclist on the cycle path. His actions in driving at less than 15mph and keeping a lookout meant he was not in breach of his duty of care. It would have been a 'counsel of perfection' to require the driver to have stopped at the intersection and edged out. The Sheriff's findings were upheld on appeal. The appellate court, on being asked to consider contributory negligence, held that had the driver been found to have had a degree of fault, the court would have assessed his contribution as 15%.

In *Clenshaw v Tanner*, the claimant was cycling in a cycle lane on the nearside of an A-road, travelling slightly faster than the cars to his offside. A breakdown recovery vehicle turned across the cycle lane into a petrol station on the nearside. A collision occurred between the claimant's bicycle and the rear of the recovery vehicle. Both parties claimed to have seen the other before the point of collision. The claimant said that the recovery vehicle was not indicating, the defendant said that it was. The court preferred the account of the defendant, finding that not only was his indicator on, but that it had been for some time before the collision, namely since it passed a bus stop 38 metres back. The court also found that the claimant was in a racing position with his head down as he approached the petrol station. Nevertheless, the defendant was found to be at fault for turning into the petrol station, crossing the dedicated cycle lane, without first checking to ensure it was safe to do so. The court specifically referred to Rule 122 of the Highway Code, which deals with the duty to give way when turning left across a cycle lane. However, the claimant was also found to be at fault – liability was apportioned 50:50 – for ignoring the defendant's signal to turn left, a signal which he ought to have seen if he had been paying proper attention.

A not uncommon occurrence, that of a parked vehicle in a cycle lane, was at issue in *Foster v Maguire* [2001] EWCA Civ 273. There a van and trailer had parked in the cycle lane of a busy dual carriageway in adverse weather conditions. It may seem unsurprising that this was found to present a possible source of danger and injury to other road users, particularly cyclists. However, the claimant had to take the issue to the Court of Appeal to secure that finding. At first instance she was held to be entirely responsible for the collision due to her own failure to look ahead. The driver of the van had switched on his hazard lights and the court found that the vehicle would have been visible to the approaching claimant cyclist for not less than one minute. On appeal, with a 2:1 majority, the court held that the van driver had created a danger from which it was reasonably foreseeable that injury could arise. Nevertheless, contributory negligence was assessed at the significant figure of 70%.

Another regular hazard, this time a car emerging from a driveway, was the issue in *Richards v Quinton* [2000] 10 WLUK 814. In order to exit his driveway and access a main road, the defendant had to cross a cycle path. As he did so, a cyclist riding along the cycle path came into collision with the vehicle. At first instance, the court split liability evenly between the parties, 50:50. The driver appealed. Whilst the driver remained partly at fault, the appellate court held that the cyclist had had a better opportunity to avoid the collision and could have acted when he saw the defendant's car emerge from the driveway. Despite the fact that the claimant was on a designated cycle path, contributory negligence was assessed on appeal at 75%. That might seem heavy-handed on the cyclist, but crucial to that analysis was that the claimant was in fact cycling contrary to the directional arrows on that cycle path.

Insurance

If a cyclist is wholly or partly at fault for an accident, are they worth suing? There's no compulsion on cyclists to have specific insurance, unlikely motorists. Nor is there any equivalent to the Motor Insurers' Bureau that can step in when a cyclist isn't insured. However, many household contents insurance policies also contain personal liability provisions. These often cover the policy holder for damage or injury caused to others outside of the home, for example in a cycling accident. These policies aren't always a complete answer though as they will always have exposure limits that mean if you are dealing with a catastrophic injury, it's unlikely to be enough. A lot of regular cyclists will be a member of an organisation like British Cycling, through which they will have liability insurance. Cycling clubs also often have their own insurance that covers club rides. Before assuming that a cyclist won't be worth suing, it is worth exploring his or her insurance position first.

CHAPTER THREE

SPORTIVES, COACHED CYCLING AND GROUP RIDES

In March 2014, British Cycling described 'cyclosportives' – commonly abbreviated to a 'sportives' – as:

> *"**non-competitive**, mass participation challenge events, typically timed on a publicised signposted route, varying in distance of approximately 40 to 100 miles. The events are designed to be a physical, personal challenge using a combination of distance and severity of the course to test the typical 200 to 5,000 participants."*
>
> (emphasis added.)

Sportives have consistently grown in popularity in the UK since 2014, offering participants a challenge that can be as gruelling or straightforward as they wish. Whilst there is an invariable emphasis from organisers that these are not races[6], results are usually published in detail on events' websites, frequently including split times and leader boards. Most sportives try to appeal to all riders, regardless of experience or fitness level, but it is a reasonable observation that many participants regard sportives as inherently competitive events, whether it be against the clock, friends or other riders taking part in the

[6] Section 31 of the Road Traffic Act 1988: Regulation of cycle racing on public ways:

(1) A person who promotes or takes part in a race or trial of speed on a public way between cycles is guilty of an offence, unless the race or trial—

(a) is authorised, and

(b) is conducted in accordance with any conditions imposed

event. This was explicitly acknowledged by HHJ Platts whilst sitting as a High Court Judge in the recent case of *Dougan v. Bike Events Limited*[7]. When analysing one of the better known sportives in the United Kingdom, "The Manchester 100" he said, at paragraph 11 of his judgment:

> *"The Manchester 100 is a non-competitive charity cycling event held each year around the roads and lanes of rural Cheshire. It takes place on open roads – that is roads that are not closed to normal traffic… It is a popular event attracting many amateur cyclists with varying degrees of cycling experience and ability. In 2016, 1,384 cyclists entered the 100-mile route and 840 the 100-kilometre route."*

Despite its "non-competitive" status, HHJ Platts went on, at paragraph 44 of his judgment, that the race organisers:

> *"…were or ought to have been aware that some participants would approach the event in a competitive spirit, either wanting to better their own previous time or a friend's time and that some would want to ride in groups even around bends.* ***That is the very nature of sportive events.****"*
>
> (emphasis added.)

So far as the Judge was concerned, it is well within an organiser's duty of care to take into account a certain level of competitive spirit amongst participants and, potentially at least, to take steps to safeguard against the heightened level of risk taking that competitiveness brings. That said, HHJ Platts was at pains to point out (at paragraph 45):

---

[7] Unreported. Heard in the Manchester Civil Justice Centre on 24 to 26 May 2021. Judgment handed down on 11 June 2021.

> *"all participants, including the claimant, were or ought to have been aware that the event was not a race, that it was held on open roads, and that it was their responsibility to ride safely in accordance with the highway code and road conditions at the time. I am satisfied that the defendant did all that was reasonably required of it in pre-event organisation to bring that to the attention of the participants."*

HHJ Platts was plainly referring to Rule 66 of the Highway Code which states:

> *"You should:*
>
> - *avoid any actions that could reduce your control of your cycle.*
> - *be considerate of the needs of other road users when riding in groups. You can ride two abreast and it can be safer to do so, particularly in larger groups or when accompanying children or less experienced riders. Be aware of drivers behind you and allow them to overtake (for example, by moving into single file or stopping) when you feel it is safe to let them do so.*
> - *not ride close behind another vehicle in case it stops suddenly.*
> - *not carry anything which will affect your balance or may get tangled up with your wheels or chain."*

Contributory negligence generally is dealt with in greater detail in chapter 6, but this case of *Dougan* underlines that the standards expected of cyclists are not suspended or reduced for sportives; and taking dangerous, careless or inconsiderate action during one can have consequences. It will be noted that in *Dougan*, it was held that if primary liability had been established, the cyclist would still have had to bear "at least" two-thirds of the blame when taking a sharp left-hand bend at 15-20mph[8] when there were warning signs in place.

In the Scottish case of *Daly v. Heeps and Markerstudy Ltd*[9], the point that participating in an event does not reduce a cyclist's responsibility for his own safety was made well. In that case, the pursuer (claimant) was a cyclist racing in a 10-mile, three-person team time trial event on open roads. The cyclist – who at the time was third in the line – managed to get passed a car at a narrow point in the road. Unfortunately, he was unable to avoid the car's trailer, which was transporting a boat. Whilst the driver was found to be primarily at fault for driving at excessive speed and not pulling over as far as he reasonably ought to have done, the cyclist was deemed to be *equally* responsible for the collision, on the basis that he too was moving too quickly. Similar to the case of *Dougan*, the Court (at paragraph 35) was critical of the cyclist ignoring signage warning of the impending hazard (the road narrowing) and considered the standard of care was the same as if the cyclist was not in competition:

> *"He ought to have been alerted to the narrowness of the road by the two signs which he had passed (but did not see, because he was not looking). The duty on the pursuer to take reasonable care for his own safety was not lessened by the fact that he was taking part in a team trial cycling event. It may well be that he chose to rely on Mr Barclay [a team mate ahead of him] to act as his "eyes and ears", and it may be that Mr Barclay should have shouted a further warning on seeing the trailer, but that does not absolve the pursuer of his duty for his own safety in a question with the defender. The*

[8] *See* paragraphs 5 and 52 (c) for the factual findings and contributory negligence respectively. It is fair to say, however, that the *obiter* analysis of contributory negligence was brief to the point of skeletal, with no reference made to any previous authorities.

[9] [2018] 1 WLIK 24. A first instance decision from the Sheriffdom of Lothian and Borders at Edinburgh.

> ***pursuer's conduct can perhaps be tested by asking what he ought to have done had he not been taking part in a cycling event but had simply been out for a recreational cycle on his own.*** *In those circumstances, he would have been keeping a proper look out, and when he saw the defender's vehicle approach, he would or ought to have slowed down, moved as far to the left as he could and, if necessary, stopped until the defender's vehicle had passed. The pursuer failed to do at least two of those things (and, like the defender, could possibly have been further to his left had he been cycling at a slower speed). I find that the pursuer, too, was negligent by virtue of his failures to reduce his speed and to keep a proper look out."* (emphasis added.)

Equally similar to the case of *Dougan,* the level of contributory negligence seems surprisingly high, especially when one considers the Mr Daly's excess speed had far less potency than that of the multi-ton 4x4 and laden trailer. As such, it may be wise to be cautious in placing too much emphasis on the liability split, particularly now, given the explicit hierarchy of vulnerability set out in the Highway Code.

It is a matter of speculation as to whether such a swingeing reduction would have been made if Mr Daly had been on his own, and not participating in an event, notwithstanding the judge's exhortation to apply the law *"by asking what [Mr Daly] ought to have done had he not been taking part in a cycling event but had simply been out for a recreational cycle on his own"*. The Court appeared to put much weight on the fact that the other cyclists managed to miss the trailer, but it must be said that they only did so by a matter inches. Given how small the gap was, and that it was found that the wide trailer was being driven too fast and was in an unreasonable road position, it might be thought that Mr Daly was just unlucky, not morally blameworthy (and certainly not to the extent that he was 50% responsible for the accident) had he been out by himself on a recreational ride.

Daly and *Dougan* are two examples of cases where it could be argued that cyclists in events are judged relatively sternly. But they do not appear to be outliers. In reviewing other cases involving group rides, it is difficult to avoid the impression that in general, cyclists partaking in these activities are viewed critically. For instance, in the case of *Sandison (AP) v. Coope*[10] the claimant / pursuer was riding a well-known route in Scotland called the "Etape Caledonia". She was doing this as part of a large group from her local cycling club. It was not a race, just an organised group ride. At the time of the accident, the group had split; and Mrs Sandison was riding with only one other person, a Mr Howard (a qualified British Cycling coach). As they went around a blind bend, at approximately 18 to 20mph, she and Mr Howard encountered two unrestrained dogs crossing the road after having been called across over by their owner. Mr Howard was able to avoid the dogs, but Mrs Sandison was not so fortunate, colliding with one and sustaining nasty facial injuries as a result. The Judge, Sheriff WM Wood, found, at paragraph 21 of his judgment that:

> *"In my opinion, the pursuer has established negligence here on the part of the defender: the defender was parked in a layby adjacent to a public road; he allowed his dog to cross the road to the other side; the defender should have been aware of the possibility of other road users, particularly in the vicinity of a blind corner; having taken no steps to ensure that the road was clear before so doing, the defender called the dog to him in the full knowledge that it would require to cross the public road in order to get to him; while there is a duty on all road users to take reasonable care for their own safety and to use roads at a safe speed that is appropriate for the road in question, it is not an absolute duty against all potential hazards.* ***The pursuer was not travelling at an unsafe speed or with any degree of recklessness.*** *Had she seen the dog, she would have been able to stop*

10 *Elaine Sandison (AP) residing in Paisley v. Thomas Coope residing in Taynuilt* [2016] SC PER 33.

> *or to slow down sufficiently to avoid any collision.* ***There is no evidence to suggest that the pursuer was using the road incorrectly in any way.*** *" (emphasis added.)*

Nevertheless, the Judge considered it appropriate to reduce her damages by 30% to reflect her contributory negligence, ostensibly because *"she accepted that she had given no warning of her impending approach and she accepted that she not moderated her speed in any way."*[11] Given the quoted finding above that Mrs Sandison was not travelling at an unsafe speed or otherwise using the road "incorrectly", it can only be surmised that the potent criticism was that she did not shout (or otherwise draw attention to herself) when approaching the bend. The judge having reminded himself at paragraph 21 that a road user does not owe an absolute duty against all potential hazards, it is striking that such a criticism and deduction was made. The obligation to shout when approaching every corner in the countryside – on the off chance an animal might be there and might respond – is curious, and it would be of interest if this line of authority was followed if a similar accident took place with a cyclist out on her own.

Indeed, there is a quite a contrast between these deductions for contributory negligence and those applied to 'normal' cyclists not engaging in an event. In *Dougan*, HHJ Platts (sitting as a High Court Judge) took the view that Mr Dougan would be "at least" two-thirds to blame for going around a corner too quickly, thereby straying over the middle of the road. In the case of *Sinclair v. Joyner*[12], however, Cox J held that an individual cyclist who had strayed across the middle of the road when negotiating a bend on a country road was only 25% to blame. Obviously, both cases have individual features which mean a direct comparison is unfair – for instance, in the case of *Sinclair* there

[11] Paragraph 25.

[12] [2015] EWHC 1800 (QB).

was no mention of signage warning that a sharp bend was up ahead – but it is a striking comparison.

Not all deductions are quite so difficult to explain, however. In the case of *Thomas v. Warwickshire County Council*[13], the claimant was cycling with 18 members of his cycling club on Gospel Oak Lane. Mr Thomas cycling near the rear of one of the groups, with cyclists in front, behind and to the right of him. Mr Thomas' bicycle hit a concrete spillage on the road, causing him to fall off his bicycle and suffer a significant head injury. The court held that the concrete spillage was the immediate cause of the accident, and the defendant was in breach of its duty under section 41 of the Highways Act 1980. However, in failing to keep a safe distance from the cyclist in front, and therefore being unable to see or react to any hazard on the road, the majority of the blame was attributed to Mr Thomas. He was deemed to be 60% at fault.

The organisers of events tend to be viewed slightly more benignly, *Dougan* being a case in point. A similar result was in the recent matter of *Comer v. South Lanarkshire Leisure and Culture Ltd*[14], which, whilst a Scottish case, provides some indication as to how a court in England & Wales is likely to view a case on similar facts[15]. The claimant was taking part in a duathlon event, organised by the defendant, who had run the event with the same route from around 2011 until 2017. Participants were asked to attend a pre-race briefing which highlighted a particularly dangerous part of the cycling route. Participants were asked to be careful, and not race through the area. During the event,

---

13 [2011] EWHC 772 (QB).

14 [2021] 7 WLUK 715

15 Not least because it fits neatly into the line of authority of cases in England and Wales dealing with outdoor activities: e.g. *Staples v. W Dorset DC* [1995] PIQR 439; *Darby v. National Trust* [2001] EWCA Civ 189; and *Tomlinson v. Congleton BC* [2003] UKHL 47.

the claimant's wheel made contact with the uneven and cracked surface that she had been warned about, and her bike went up in the air, with her head hitting the ground. There was no suggestion that she had been racing through the area (i.e. she had been following the guidance), but it was held that the defendant race-organisers had not breached their duty of care: they had taken sufficient and reasonable precautions in highlighting the potential problem in the pre-race briefing.

It is worth noting that the Judge, Sheriff K J Campbell QC, made the *obiter* comment at paragraphs 101 and 102 of his judgment that in the event that the defendant had been liable, no blame would have been attributed to the claimant.

In summary, therefore, Courts appear ready to emphasise an individual's responsibility when undertaking sportives or other group cycling events and recognise that not every accident can be attributed to (or solely attributed to) the event organiser or occupier. This would appear to be very much in line with authorities dealing with other outdoor activities[16].

The same level of sufferance is not afforded, however, to companies which train or coach participants as they are viewed as having assumed a greater level of responsibility for their clients. The case of *Ahmed v. MacLean*[17] is one such illustration. In that instance, Mr Ahmed undertook a beginner's mountain biking course with the defendant. Baker J, who heard the case, remarked at paragraph 73 of his judgment Mr Ahmed was a "relatively relaxed and easy-going" individual who "didn't appear to be seeking a thrilling day out" when he booked the course; "rather his aim was to ensure that he could pursue this recreation in a safe and effective manner." Unfortunately, the tuition

---

16 *ibid.*

17 [2016] EWHC 2798 (QB).

Mr Ahmed received was, at best, rudimentary, and on his second attempt to go downhill off-road, he fell over his handlebars and sustained severe injuries rendering him paraplegic. Baker J found that the instructor's assessment of Mr Ahmed's proficiency was insufficient; he failed to provide adequate instruction or demonstration; and he permitted Mr Ahmed to descend a hill that was well beyond his experience. As a result he had breached the duty of care he owed to Mr Ahmed.[18]

In terms of contributory negligence, Baker J drew heavily on the case of *Anderson v. Lyotier*[19]:

> *"... In that case the claimant, who was taking part in a mixed ability skiing lesson run by the defendant, was seriously injured when the defendant took the group down an off-piste section without having properly ascertained that the claimant could traverse the slope in safety. Foskett J. found that, although the defendant was mostly to blame for the accident, the claimant also bore some responsibility on the basis that, either knowing that he lacked the ability to ski down the slope in safety, or at least feeling sufficiently concerned for his safety as to warrant notifying the defendant about it, he failed to notify the defendant about it.*
>
> *In the course of his judgment at paragraph 142 Foskett J. said,*
>
> > *"... The process involving adults must be a collaborative one. I do not think that the law requires (and, if it did, for my part I would say that it would be adopting the wrong policy) that the instructor takes total responsibility in a situation such as that which obtained in this case. In my judgment, if an instructor does suggest something to a skier under his*

18 Paragraphs 81 to 84.

19 [2008] EWHC 2790 (QB). The cited passage starts at paragraph 99 of Baker J's judgment.

> *supervision that the skier believes to be beyond what it is reasonable for him to attempt, there is an onus on the skier to say so....I do not consider it is, objectively speaking, reasonable for the skier not to say something in that situation. The human reaction not to want to appear awkward, difficult or, as Mr Foxon put it, "faint-hearted" is quite understandable from a subjective viewpoint; but objective analysis does suggest that serious concerns must be ventilated."*

I respectfully agree with the views expressed by Foskett J., and consider that there are sufficient similarities between the challenges faced by those involved in skiing and mountain biking, that, at least with adults, the nature of the relationship between the trainer and trainee is analogous. Therefore, in the present case, I consider that just as the defendant owed a duty of care to the claimant, so too did the claimant bear some responsibility for his own safety.

.... I appreciate that, in so far as mountain bike skills were concerned, the claimant was a novice. However, I do not consider that this would entirely preclude the claimant's appreciation of his ability to ride down the slope in safety, nor do I consider that it entitled him to abdicate complete responsibility for his own safety. The claimant is an adult, and it is of relevance that he had been riding a mountain bike for a number of years, albeit on less challenging terrain, and would therefore have some appreciation of his own ability to meet the challenge presented by the slope in question. Indeed, it is of significance that the claimant's injury occurred during his second descent down the slope, rather than the first during which he would have gained further insight into his inability to descend the slope in safety, not least from his initial fall.

It is also pointed out on behalf of the claimant that, after his first descent down the slope, not only did the defendant inform the claimant that his technique was OK, but he also advised the claimant that on his next descent he should ride down the slope at

> *greater speed. It is argued on behalf of the claimant that these matters would have provided him with a wholly misleading impression as to his ability to ride down the slope with safety, and thus deprived the claimant of the opportunity of making an appropriate reassessment of his own ability to descend the slope on the second occasion. Although, I accept that these two matters would have been likely to have provided a measure of false reassurance to the claimant as to his ability to ride down the slope again in safety, I do not consider that they had the effect of totally eclipsing the claimant's responsibility for his own safety, in that despite them he would have retained some insight into his own abilities. However, due to the fact that there was some measure of false reassurance, I do consider that these matters are of relevance to the apportionment of liability between the parties, and they have led me to a slightly different determination upon this issue than that considered appropriate in the circumstances of the Anderson case.*
>
> *Accordingly, and in order to seek to reflect these matters, I consider that the appropriate amount of responsibility which the claimant should bear in relation to his contribution to the cause of this accident is one of 20%."*

There was also some interesting *obiter dicta* at paragraph 76 of the decision. Although one could be critical of Mr Ahmed, especially because he was a lawyer, for not having properly read either the terms and conditions on the website or the pre-ride safety check list, none of the participants gave evidence that they had read the terms, nor that they expressly recalled the defendant pointing out to them that, if they had any doubts, they could get off their bikes and walk. In short, a defendant's ability to shift further responsibility onto a paying client by use of written terms and conditions may be hard pressed.

As a final thought in relation to the approach to risk in amateur "non"-competitions, it has been reported that there has been a significant rise in doping cases within sportives[20]. However, it is hard to imagine this amounting to a relevant factor in an accident, unless the drug somehow rendered the cyclist incapable of having proper control of the bicycle – in which case it might amount to a criminal offence as well as a contributing factor in any civil litigation[21]). There are some anecdotal stories in relation to the use of painkillers inhibiting a cyclist's ability to control a bike, but it is hard to see a successful argument that an event-organiser ought to take steps to try and control this sort of behaviour.

---

20 For instance: https://www.theguardian.com/lifeandstyle/2016/jun/01/dope-and-glory-the-rise-of-cheating-in-amateur-sport

21 Section 30 of the Road Traffic Act 1988 makes it explicit that the offence of cycling under the influence of drugs is only committed if the influence of the drug rendered the cyclist "incapable of having proper control of the cycle".

CHAPTER FOUR

PROFESSIONAL CYCLING

Reported cases involving professional cyclists are very few and far between. They tend to be either contractual disputes (such as employment status like *Varnish v. British Cycling Federation*[22]); doping allegations; or injuries that have occurred outside of competition, usually whilst training. This chapter, therefore, is not a long one. It is hoped, however, that it is still useful in terms of highlighting some of the salient issues surrounding civil claims. Doping and other aspects of the sport of cycling regulated by the national and international governing bodies are not dealt with here.

In terms of establishing a breach of a duty of care by a competitor, it is suggested that the most useful, recent authority is that of *Tylicki v. Gibbons*[23] which, whilst dealing with injuries in a horse race, sets out a number of principles applicable to bicycle racing not least because of the similarity of the sports and the inherent risks both involve. Both Mr Tylicki and Mr Gibbons were successful and experienced professional flat race jockeys. During a race held at Kempton at Halloween in 2016, there was a collision between their respective horses, which caused Mr Tylicki to fall with devastating results – he broke his neck causing complete paraplegia. At trial, Mr Gibbons accepted (as he was bound to do) that when racing, each jockey had a duty of care to the others. The issues in dispute were what standard duty of care is and whether it was breached on this occasion, with Mr Gibbons placing considerable reliance on the fact that this was

---

22 [2020] 5 WLUK 539.

23 [2021] EWHC 3470 (QB)

considered merely a racing incident at the Stewards Enquiry[24] following the accident.

HHJ Walden-Smith (sitting as a High Court Judge) reminded herself, at paragraphs 23 to 24 of her judgment, of the following, before making her findings:

> "*...the leading authority applicable to this claim is* Peter Harvey Caldwell v (1) Adrian Maguire
>
> and (2) Mick Fitzgerald *[2001] EWCA Civ 1054.*
>
> Caldwell *establishes several important principles. It is necessary, however, to recognise that... [each case should be] determined on its own particular facts:*
>
>> *"In an action for damages by one participant in a sporting contest against another participant in the same game or event, the issue of negligence cannot be resolved in a vacuum. It is fact specific." (per Judge LJ, as he then was, at paragraph 30 of Caldwell).*

In relation to the 'important principles' established by Caldwell, she continued:

(a) Breaching rules of a sport does not automatically establish liability in negligence.

(b) By engaging in a sport, participants may be held to have accepted risks which are inherent in it but that does not eliminate all duty of care of the one participant to the other.

---

[24] Cycling has similar arbiters in sports, commonly referred to as 'commissaires'.

(c) The duty is to exercise all care that is "objectively reasonable" in the prevailing circumstances to avoid injuring fellow contestants.

(d) The "prevailing circumstances" encompass all relevant issues, including (but not necessarily limited to): the object of the contest, the demands inevitably made upon its contestants, the sport's inherent dangers, its rules, conventions and customs, and the standards, skills and judgment reasonably to be expected of a contestant.

(e) The threshold for liability in professional horse racing (and, it is suggested, professional cycling) is, in practice, inevitably high; and the proof of a breach of duty will not flow from proof a mere error of judgment or momentary lapse in skill. These should be viewed simply as incidents inherent in the nature of the sport.

(f) In practice it may therefore be difficult to prove breach of duty absent proof of conduct that amounts to reckless disregard for the fellow contestant's safety. This is not the same as saying that a claimant needs to establish "recklessness" in order to succeed, but it is an acknowledgment that there is a higher bar than a mere error of judgment in the context of a fast-moving contest.

HHJ Walden-Smith went on to expand this point (f) at paragraph 75 of her judgment:

> "*…In effect, while recklessness has been expressly stated not to be the test for a finding of negligence,* ***in effect the evidential burden is such that requires a reckless disregard for the safety of others.*** *Of course, in placing the threshold at that high level, regard is being had to all the circumstances of the sport, the inherent dangers and the high degree of competitiveness with a requirement on jockeys to*

> *win or be best placed. The fact that the threshold is high does not mean, however, that no duty of care is owed between jockeys."* (emphasis added.)

In the end, HHJ Walden-Smith considered that despite this high threshold, in this particular incident, Mr Gibbons had indeed breached his duty of care to Mr Tylicki, cutting across his racing line when he knew or ought to have known that in doing so, he was endangering Mr Tylicki and his horse. The manoeuvre, known as "closing the door", is one that is often seen to varying degrees in cycle race sprinting, to the extent that it is anticipated that this case will be cited in potential cycling cases in the future.

Two other aspects of the judgment are worth noting. Firstly, the judge was sympathetic to the Stewards who looked into the incident immediately afterwards, but considered their investigation flawed, their conclusions wrong, and, in any event, not binding on her[25]. As she said at paragraph 50 of her judgment: *"The evidence of the Stewards merely forms one part of [the] evidence"*. It seems obvious that a court would have a similar discretion to come to a different conclusion to one made by cycling commissaires following any incident.

Secondly, at paragraphs 32 and 33, HHJ Walden-Smith explicitly rejected the argument that claims arising from sporting contests should be dismissed (except in exceptional circumstances) in order to avoid litigation "floodgates" opening and claims proliferating. This is undoubtedly the correct approach, and thus far at least, there does not appear to be any realistic basis for concern.

One potential barrier to claiming, however, may be the absence of a paymaster. Whilst most professional cyclists will have the appropriate insurance to meet any claim made against them, even if there is no direct employer, it is worth noting that not all professional cyclists are

[25] Paragraphs 44 & 50 to 55.

employed so there may be a pitfall in considering a claim based on vicarious liability. Whilst not directly a case on point, the issue of employment status was explored fully in the matter of *Varnish* (cited above). In that employment case, the very successful professional cyclist Jessica Varnish was deemed by the Employment Appeal Tribunal not to be an employee of or worker for the British Cycling Federation within the meaning of section 230 of the Employment rights Act 1996.

Section 230 of the 1996 Act provides:

> (1) In this Act "employee" means an individual who has entered into or works under (or, where the employment has ceased, worked under) a contract of employment.
>
> (2) In this Act "contract of employment" means a contract of service or apprenticeship, whether express or implied, and (if it is express) whether oral or in writing.
>
> (3) In this Act "worker" (except in the phrases "shop worker" and "betting worker") means an individual who has entered into or works under (or, where the employment has ceased, worked under) –
>
> > (a) a contract of employment, or
> >
> > (b) any other contract, whether express or implied and (if it is express) whether oral or in writing, whereby the individual undertakes to do or perform personally any work or services for another party to the contract whose status is not by virtue of the contract that of a client or customer of any profession or business undertaking carried on by the individual;

and any reference to a worker's contract shall be construed accordingly.

(4) In this Act "employer", in relation to an employee or a worker, means the person by whom the employee or worker is (or, where the employment has ceased, was) employed.

(5) In this Act "employment"–

(a) in relation to an employee, means (except for the purposes of section 171) employment under a contract of employment, and

(b) in relation to a worker, means employment under his contract; and "employed" shall be construed accordingly."

The EAT upheld the first instance decision that the relationship between the two parties was one which allowed Ms Varnish to avail herself of various services British Cycling provided, if she chose to do so, in order to achieve their joint aim of winning medals at international level. It did not amount to anything more. British Cycling did not pay her; and she was free to choose her own coach and (in some circumstances her own equipment) if she wished. The money she received was a non-repayable grant from a different sports body, UK Sport, and this funding was not based on work done but on future potential. In short, British Cycling was the institution which provided her with training facilities and opportunities, but this did not translate into an employer/employee relationship or even a business/worker relationship. Whilst clunky (and the EAT was not quick to adopt it as an analogy) there was a certain similarity with a student attending university – the student was there to train and flourish but that did not translate into a greater mutuality of obligations which created a contractual relationship amounting to employment. The EAT went on to say, however, at paragraph 49 of its judgment:

> *"…The Tribunal's conclusion [which it upheld] does not mean that in another case, where perhaps the contractual provisions, and the balance between services provided to and performed by the athlete, are different, the training done by a cyclist could not be found to amount to work. The legislation does not seek to define what is meant by "work" or "service". The constantly evolving nature of what is regarded as amounting to work or service would probably make such definition impossible, or at least liable to be quickly outmoded. Not all work will be of the kind that gives rise to an employment relationship; the hard-working student at university is a possible example of that. It is left to the Tribunal, having found that there is a contract, to consider all the relevant factors (including the nature of the work done) and assess whether the contract is one of service or not."*

In terms of quantum, there is nothing unique about claims by professional cyclists following injury. The usual rules regarding remoteness and a claimant's duty to mitigate apply; and – as with all claims for lost earnings from professional sporting endeavour – calculating the lost opportunities is usually one of the central issues in the case.

Expert evidence will often be crucial, with cycling agents specialising in the relevant area of cycling (for instance, road racers; mountain bikers or track cyclists) being considered the best starting point for setting out the various issues, including the likely level of salary an athlete might expect but for their accident; bonus structures; prize money (including how that is shared[26]); taxation; agent fees; and

[26] This can vary between disciplines, with the convention in some parts of the sport being that any such money is pooled and distributed amongst the team. Whether this convention is adhered to unstintingly will be a matter of evidence; but, of

collateral contracts such as sponsorship deals with brands and/or whether equipment can be kept by an athlete. The pool of agents, however, is small, and some are less prepared to provide specifics than others. In as far as it needed saying, witnesses of fact (e.g. former cyclists or current team mates) are also crucial in evidencing the injured cyclist's prospects.

course, it could supplement the income of a more minor rider if they are on a team with one or two big stars.

CHAPTER FIVE

HIGHWAYS CASES

The remedy in respect of a breach of a highway authority's duty to maintain the highway is founded upon a breach of statutory duty and not upon the tort of negligence. Section 41 of the Highways Act 1980 imposes a duty on highways authorities to maintain the highway. The duty is to maintain the structure and fabric of the highway. This includes both the surface of the highway and drains associated with it. Road furniture such as manholes are the responsibility of whichever statutory authority owns them (e.g. a water company).

An important distinction is made between the surface of the highway itself and things upon it. Plants like mosses and algae growing upon a highway are not part of the structure or fabric of the highway and so there is no duty to remove them (see *Rollinson v Dudley MBC* [2015] EWHC 3330 (QB)). Ice and snow, however, although not part of the structure or fabric of the highway are something which the highway authority has a duty to address. Thanks to an amendment to section 41 brought in by section 11 of the Railway and Transport Safety Act 2003, there is a duty on a highway authority to ensure that "*so far as is reasonably practicable, safe passage along a highway is not endangered by snow and ice*". That duty is not strict, but it is onerous. A highway authority that has failed to take reasonably practicable steps to address snow or ice may not then argue that the highway was likely to be endangered by snow and ice even if such steps had been taken (*Smithson v Lynn* [2020] EWHC 2517 (QB), at [68]). Indeed, the burden of proving that it is not reasonably practicable to grit a highway falls on the highway authority (*Smithson v Lynn* [2020] EWHC 2517 (QB)). Ice and snow are exceptions to the general rule that the highway authority is not liable for transient hazards, such as mud or grit. Indeed, it was held in *Valentine v Transport for London* [2010] EWCA Civ 1358 that a failure to remove surface grit and gravel from a road did not give rise to a breach of s.41 of the 1980 Act.

As set out by Steyn LJ in *Mills v Barnsley Metropolitan Borough Council* [1992] PIQR P291 (at P292-P293), for a claimant to succeed in bringing a claim against a highway authority for an accident, the claimant must prove that:

(1) The highway was dangerous in the sense that danger could be reasonably anticipated from its use;

(2) The dangerous condition was created by the failure to maintain or repair the highway; and

(3) The injury or damage resulted from such a failure.

This involves a careful analysis of the particular facts of each case. Things such as the precise location on the road of the danger / defect and how much traffic and of what sort there usually is on that highway will be relevant.

Accordingly, there are no hard and fast rules about what will be considered an actionable danger and what will not. A 25mm deep pothole near the central white line on a rarely used country road might not be an actionable danger, whereas the same pothole on a pedestrian crossing outside an old people's home might be.

A lesser known, but occasionally pertinent, fact is that the duty owed pursuant to section 41 exists alongside duties owed by the providers of tramways where tram tracks are inserted into a road (see *Roe v Sheffield County Council (No.1)* [2003] EWCA Civ 01; [2004] QB 653).

If a breach of section 41 is made out, there is a defence open to highways authorities. Section 58 of the Act provides that it is a defence for a highway authority to prove that it had taken such care as in all the circumstances was reasonably required to ensure that the relevant part of the highway was not dangerous to traffic. In order to establish the defence, the highway authority must satisfy the court on these five factors, as set out in section 58(2):

(1) The character of the highway and the traffic which was reasonably expected to use it;

(2) The standard of maintenance appropriate to the highway;

(3) The state of repair in which a reasonable person would have expected to find the highway;

(4) Whether the highway authority knew or ought to have known that the condition of the relevant part of the highway was likely to cause danger to users of the highway; and

(5) Where the highway authority could not reasonably have been expected to repair the highway before the index accident, what warning notices of its condition had been displayed.

Importantly, it is of no assistance to a highway authority to plead that financial constraints prevented them from taking the necessary steps (see *Wilkinson v York CC* [2011] EWCA Civ 207). Nor is it a defence for a highway authority to prove that it has arranged for a competent third party to carry out the maintenance of the highway, unless it is also proved that it has given that third party proper instructions concerning the maintenance, and the third party has carried them out.

There is a code of good practice for highway maintenance, published by the Local Authorities Association. This code can be a useful reference point as a guide to what might – or might not – be a breach of section 41. Indeed, many highways authorities have adopted its recommendations. Nevertheless, the code remains mere guidance, it is not mandatory. In any highways case, it is worth taking time to understand the code and the relationship between it and the particular defendant's own policy of inspection.

The overall legal analysis boils down to three questions:

(1) What caused the accident? (Factual causation)

(2) Was what caused the accident a danger? (Section 41 of the Highways Act 1980)

(3) Did the highway authority take reasonable steps to mitigate the danger / avoid the accident? (Section 58 of the Highways Act 1980)

Case Examples and Tips

In *Griffiths v Gwynedd CC* [2015] EWCA Civ 1440, the claimant, Mr Griffiths, was cycling along a country road when he had an accident as a result of cycling over a pothole. The road was described as a remote mountain road. It was inspected twice a year. The relevant pothole was "*at least 80mm in depth*" and had been caused by the wearing away of the wearing (i.e. surface) course of the tarmac, exposing the base course.

At first instance, the judge found that the pothole was visible from some 21 metres away, that it was by the very edge of the road. It was also found that the claimant came upon the pothole because of the peculiar circumstance that he swerved to avoid some stones and manure. The judge found that this pothole was not a breach of section 41. The claimant appealed to the Court of Appeal.

The appeal was rejected. The Court of Appeal reiterated the relevance of the nature of the road and the extent of its use by persons in the same category as the claimant, i.e. cyclists, when analysing the defect's dangerousness. Accordingly, a "*defect on a remote rural mountain road, which was a wholly unremarkable and commonplace feature of such a location, could in the ordinary course of human affairs be regarded as something that was not properly classified as a danger to the persons who were likely to use it*" (at paragraph 34).

An interesting point in *Griffiths* was that neither the claimant, who regularly cycled this route, nor a local who was also aware of the pothole, had reported it to the highway authority. Early disclosure by a highway authority of any reports – or lack thereof – of a defect at the relevant location and what, if anything, was ordered or done about it, can be extremely helpful. Indeed, claimants would do well to themselves report the defect after their accident. Else it is left open to a defendant to suggest that the claimant him/herself didn't even consider the defect sufficiently dangerous to be worth reporting. It is also worth being careful to take time to properly understand a highways authority's records and what different inspections entail, why and when they might be ad hoc as opposed to scheduled, how roads are classified, etc.

Hilliard v Surrey County Council [2018] EWHC 3156 (QB) was a case arising from an accident that occurred during a closed road sportif, Ride London. The claimant had suffered personal injury in an accident as a result of a depression in the road that was adjacent to a water hydrant cover. The District Judge who heard the case at first instance found the highways authority liable under section 41. The highways authority appealed. The case is worth reading in full, but some aspects of how the court handled the evidence are of particular note.

At the time of the accident, some 12,400 cyclists had passed over the defect. Although the District Judge had referred to this, he did not set out any analysis as to if or how he had taken it into account in his conclusion. The appellate court considered that this fact was important, indeed overwhelming, evidence in determining whether the road was dangerous (see paragraph 46). That gives a helpful reminder of how in highways cases the relevant defect needs to be dangerous to be actionable. It is not enough that a defect simply could foreseeably cause an accident or injury. However, the appellate court described the evidence of the 12,400 earlier cyclists passing "*without incident*" is perhaps overstating the evidence. The fact that no accidents had been reported does not mean that there were no incidents, i.e. no near misses, no last minute 'bunny hop' manoeuvres over the defect, no crashes or falls but without reported injury. Indeed, in considering the 12,400 cyclists it is also worth remembering that this sportif was taking place on closed roads. The cyclists had the full width of the road at their disposal and so may have been better placed to avoid the defect than they would have been in usual circumstances on open roads.

Further, the appellate court criticised the District Judge for having given undue weight to a description of the defect as a "*trip hazard*" in a report prepared for another purpose, namely at the request of Thames Water following a section 81 notice. Mrs Justice Slade, hearing the appeal, held that whilst the report "*made an observation that the defect would have been a trip hazard for pedestrians, that is not the test to be applied by the judge in determining whether the road was reasonably passable to ordinary traffic of the neighbourhood without danger caused by its physical condition*". Again, perhaps more nuance was required here. Whilst a pedestrian trip hazard might not render a highway dangerous to ordinary motor vehicle traffic, such a hazard is exactly the sort of defect that could cause a cyclist on narrow road tyres to come a cropper. This accident occurred on a well-ridden route in Surrey, so the "*ordinary traffic of the neighbourhood*" should have included road cyclists, such as the claimant. Nevertheless, the appeal was allowed and the claim was dismissed as it was held that section 41 was not made out.

When faced with determining the "*ordinary traffic*" at an accident locus, modern technology can be extremely helpful. Many cyclists these days use technology such as Strava as well as devices like Garmins and Wahoos, which record their routes and their speeds. Many of these pieces of software also collate the data. Strava, for example, has a "heat map" function, which allows a subscriber to plot a route based on which routes other cyclists take in that area, with an indication given on a map of how popular different routes are. This is a potentially important source of information for indicating how frequently or infrequently a particular road is ridden by cyclists.

Both *Nash v Hertfordshire County Council* [2020] EWHC 3247 (QB) and *Walsh v The Council of the Borough of Kirklees* [2019] EWHC 491 (QB) contain helpful summaries of the law on defects in the highways. Their greatest use, perhaps, though is to emphasise the importance of photographs in any highways claim. If either party is advancing a case based on the relevant defect being of a particular length, width or depth, that needs to be evidenced. Else, as the judge in *Nash* (at paragraph 13) quoted from the judge in *Walsh*, "*there is in my judgment simply not enough reliable evidence of the dimensions or conditions of the pothole for me to say it is more likely than not that it presented a real source of danger in the sense identified in Mills…*". The simplest and best way to evidence the dimensions of a defect is to photograph it with a spirit level, a gradient gauge, and a measuring tape or ruler.

CHAPTER SIX

CONTRIBUTORY NEGLIGENCE

In accidents between road users, contributory negligence is often put in issue. With claims involving cyclists, it can extend beyond allegations about their cycling to contentions about their clothing, lights, whether or not they were wearing a helmet, and so on.

Although contributory negligence does not depend on a breach of duty to the defendant (likely another road user), it does depend on foreseeability. Contributory negligence requires foreseeability of harm to oneself. A person is liable for contributory negligence whenever he or she ought reasonably to have foreseen that, if he or she did not act prudently, he or she might suffer injury. As part of that foreseeability analysis, he or she should take into account the possibility of others being careless.

The basis of the partial defence of contributory negligence is section 1(1) of the Law Reform (Contributory Negligence) Act 1945. The assessment of any contributory negligence involves two factors:

(1) Blameworthiness; and

(2) Causative potency.

A helpful example of an analysis of these factors can be found in the case of *McGeer v Macintosh* [2017] EWCA Civ 79, which involved an HGV turning left at traffic lights with a cyclist on its nearside.

As set out earlier in the book, a breach of the Highway Code does not of itself evidence negligence (or indeed a criminal offence), but nevertheless it can be relied upon in an effort to establish liability. The Code contains numerous provisions relevant to cyclists that may inform whether or not they might be considered contributorily negligent in an accident. The key provisions are those found in **Rules 59 to 82**.

Rule 59 on clothing and helmets is advisory, not mandatory. **Rule 60** on lights and reflectors, however, is mandatory. Accordingly, a court is likely to be readier to find a failure to have bike lights at night to be contributorily negligent than a failure to wear high-vis clothing, although all factors influencing a cyclist's visibility should properly be considered. The issue of helmets is dealt with in more detail in a later chapter.

Much of the jurisprudence dealing with contributory negligence in cycling cases involves similar issues and analysis to those seen in accidents involving motor vehicles: speed, road positioning, keeping a lookout, etc. The handful of cases below are ones that look at issues of contributory negligence that are more specific to cycling cases than road traffic cases more generally.

Despite the mandatory wording of **Rule 60**, not displaying lights at night will not always result in a reduction for contributory negligence, as shown in *Phethean-Hubble v Coles* [2012] EWCA Civ 349; [2011] EWHC 363 (QB). The claimant had been cycling along a pavement before turning into the road by "bunny-hopping" at an angle of some 25-30 degrees, where he was then struck by a car driven by the defendant. The defendant was found to have been driving too fast and so primary liability attached. However, the claimant was not using lights on his bike, nor was he wearing a helmet. Interestingly, the first instance judge (at paragraph 114) stated that the defendant, "*saw a cyclist who was not displaying lights and who therefore may not be so mindful to take such care of his own safety, that the motorist could rely upon his not coming into the road*". That appears to put a greater onus on the driver to be careful when faced with an apparently reckless cyclist. Yet the judge went on to find that, "*The fact that the Claimant had no rear light has very limited relevance in this case since the road was well lit and the Defendant accepts that he saw the Claimant riding along the pavement in any event and had no difficulty in seeing him*" (at paragraph 128). The judge also dismissed the claimant's lack of helmet as irrelevant on the facts. He did, however, conclude that there was contributory negligence on the part of the claimant for creating an emergency situation by leaving the pavement as he did. The judge said that his starting point for such contributory negligence was 50%, but he would reduce it to a third to account for the claimant's young age, 16. That reduction was reversed on appeal and 50% imposed since there was no good reason not to treat the cyclist as an adult.

In *Clenshaw v Tanner*, also dealt with earlier in this book, liability was apportioned between the claimant cyclist and the defendant recovery truck driver 50:50. The claimant had been cycling in a cycle lane on the nearside of an A-road. A breakdown recovery vehicle turned across the cycle lane into a petrol station on the nearside. A collision occurred between the claimant's bicycle and the rear of the recovery vehicle. The court also found that the claimant was in a racing position with his head down as he approached the petrol station. He was found to have been contributorily negligent for ignoring the defendant's signal to turn left, a signal which he ought to have seen if he had had his head up and been paying proper attention.

The case of *Foster v Maguire* [2001] EWCA Civ 273 stands as another warning to cyclists of the importance of keeping a lookout, even when in cycle lanes. There, contributory negligence was assessed at the significant figure of 70% when a claimant cyclist rode into a van and trailer that had parked in the cycle lane of a busy dual carriageway in adverse weather conditions. The driver of the van had switched on his hazard lights and the court found that the vehicle would have been visible to the approaching claimant cyclist for not less than one minute.

A more favourable case for cyclists is that of *Kotula v EDF Energy Networks (EPN) Plc* [2010] 6 WLUK 234. In that case, contributory negligence was dealt with as a preliminary issue, primary liability having been conceded. The facts were that the claimant cyclist had fallen in front of a lorry whilst navigating through a traffic management system erected around the defendant's excavation in a pavement alongside a busy urban road. The defendant alleged contributory negligence in the claimant either riding his bicycle through the street works or for carelessly walking through them (rather than using an alternative pavement). Judge Simon Brown QC appeared to have no difficulty in dispensing with each alternative. He determined the matter in favour of the claimant entirely, finding that the defendant had laid "*out a very hazardous multi-layered trap of a narrow path on a curve with a kerb across it for <u>all</u> pedestrians, including those just on foot, with children, with buggies, cycles, or prams besides a very busy road with no warnings and no safety zone between the barrier in the road and large lorries travelling lawfully along the road*" (paragraph 48, original emphasis).

Thomas v Warwickshire CC [2011] EWHC 772 (QB) dealt with contributory negligence where a cyclist had been part of a chain gang when he sustained a significant head injury after hitting a spillage of concrete on the road. The claimant was an experienced cyclist who had been cycling as part of a group of approximately 20 cyclists, riding in ranks of two, travelling at 20-25mph. The claimant's evidence was that he had been riding about 5 to 6 inches behind the back wheel of the rider in front. The judge held that, "*If he had been travelling at a safe distance from the cyclist in front he would have been able to see what was coming up in sufficient time to have made the minor adjustment to his course which would have enabled him to avoid running into or over the concrete spillage*" (at paragraph 92). As a result, contributory negligence of 60% was applied: a salutary warning to cyclists riding in chain-gangs, perhaps.

A question often asked is whether it is contributorily negligent to ride a bicycle whilst drunk. It is an offence under the Road Traffic Act 1988 to ride a bicycle whilst under the influence of drink or drugs (cycling offences are set out at sections 28 to 32 of the Act). However, when it comes to contributory negligence, the mere fact of being drunk won't automatically qualify. Rather, a cyclist's actual behaviour as a road user needs to be negligent, such as veering into the road or failing to keep a lookout. Although involving a drunk pedestrian, rather than a drunk cyclist, the point is illustrated well by the case of *Wooldridge v George* [2017] EWHC 332 (QB). Nonetheless, a court is perhaps more likely to find as a fact that a cyclist had indeed exhibited negligent behaviour as a road user if that cyclist was drunk at the time.

CHAPTER SEVEN

CYCLE HELMETS

The obligation to wear a cycle helmet has been one that has exercised many over the years. Repeated draft bills have come before Parliament with the intention of mandating their use by children[27] and outside Parliament and the Courts, cycle helmets seem to generate fiercely polarised standpoints. Putting the soapbox rhetoric to one side, however the seminal case regarding their use is *Smith v. Finch*[28] from 2009.

Mr Smith was knocked from his bicycle by a motorbike which had been driven at speed by Mr Finch. Mr Smith's head struck a raised kerb at the side of the road and as a consequence, he sustained serious head injuries including an extradural haematoma, occipital fractures, and traumatic subarachnoid and cerebral haemorrhages. He had to undergo a temporal craniotomy and lobectomy and have his inferior frontal lobe removed. The result was devastating for Mr Smith. His cognition, behaviour, and speech function were all grossly affected; he required help with everyday tasks; and he developed post traumatic epilepsy.

At trial, Griffith Williams J determined that the accident was solely caused by Mr Finch. He went on to consider, however, whether Mr Smith's damages should be reduced to account for the fact that he was not wearing a helmet. The salient passage of his judgment is worth citing in full:

---

[27] For instance, in 2004 and 2007.

[28] [2009] EWHC 53 QB.

"43. I remind myself that I am concerned to decide what standard of care should have been required of a pedal cyclist in 2005. My conclusion is that the study by Inwood, Whitely and Sexton in 2004 [cited earlier in the judgment]… does not support an argument that as the majority then was not using helmets, it would be wrong to impose a requirement that they should be worn. As it is accepted that the wearing of helmets may afford protection in some circumstances, it must follow that ***a cyclist of ordinary prudence would wear one, no matter whether on a long or a short trip or whether on quiet suburban roads or a busy main road****. The introduction to the Highway Code stated that "Knowing and applying the rules contained in the Highway Code could significantly reduce road accident casualties. Cutting the number of deaths and injuries that occur on our roads every day is the responsibility we all share".*

44. In my judgment the observations of Lord Denning MR in <u>Froom and others v. Butcher</u> *[cited at length earlier in the judgment][29]… should apply to the wearing of helmets by cyclists. It matters not that there is no legal compulsion for cyclists to wear helmets and so a cyclist is free to choose whether or not to wear one because there can be no doubt that the failure to wear a helmet may expose the cyclist to the risk of greater injury; such a failure would not be "a sensible thing to do" and so, subject to issues of causation, any injury sustained may be the cyclist's own fault and "he has only himself to thank for the consequences".*

[29] [1976] 1 QB 286. This case is considered the leading authority in relation to contributory negligence for failing to wear a seatbelt in a car.

45. *I am satisfied on the balance of probabilities, that the cyclist who does not wear a helmet runs the risk of contributing to his/her injuries....*

46. ***That said, the burden is on the Defendant to prove*** *(i) that the Claimant failed to take ordinary care of himself, or in other words, to take such care as a reasonable man would take for his own safety by not wearing a helmet and (ii)* ***that his failure was a contributory cause of the damage*** – Lewis –v- Denye *[1939] 1 KB 540 at 554 per Parcq LJ... " (emphasis added).*

Applying that analysis to the evidence before him, Griffith Williams J found:

(a) He was not satisfied that the speed of the accident was slow enough for a helmet to have made a difference (para. 53). From the expert evidence that was before him, he considered that any accident in excess of 12mph was likely to render a helmet otiose.

(b) In any event, the scalloped design at the back of the helmet did not afford any protection to the lower part of the back of Mr Smith's head, and there was a "real possibility" that it was this which struck the raised kerb (para. 53).

(c) The Defendant had failed to show that an approved helmet would have prevented or made less severe the head injuries sustained by Mr Smith (paras. 54 and 55).

(d) He "could not exclude as a possibility" that even if the impact was at a low enough speed for a helmet to afford some protection, Mr Smith's more serious injuries were caused by a contre-coup injury – an injury from which a helmet would not have protected the Claimant (para. 56).

In short, whilst wearing a cycle helmet is a prudent safety measure in principle, the difference it is likely to make is much harder to gauge. Time and again, the point has been pleaded in a Defence, only for the matter to be abandoned at or before trial because it is accepted by the Defendant that it cannot prove it would have made a material difference – *see*, for instance: *Sinclair v. Joyner*; *Foulds v. Devon CC*; *Malasi v. Ahmed*; and *Wakeling v. Mc Donagh*[30].

Smith v. Finch is also notable for three further reasons. Firstly, as Griffith Williams J pointed out at paragraph 55 of his judgment, it was a "fundamental evidential omission" by the Defendant not to adduce any medical evidence in support of the contention Mr Smith's injuries would not have occurred or would be less serious.

Secondly, Griffith Williams J leant heavily on the authority of *Froom v. Butcher* as justification for the finding that in principle, a reduction for contributory negligence would be appropriate. He was silent, however, on whether he would have adopted the same percentages as those used in *Froom* for a failure to wear a seatbelt, namely 25% if all injuries were avoided; and 15% if the severity of injury would have been reduced. On the one hand, in citing so extensively from *Froom*, including the passage by Lord Denning MR which mentioned the figures, it may be assumed that these were the sort of reductions Griffith Williams J considered apposite. However, it could also be argued that a failure to wear a seatbelt is more egregious and therefore a smaller deduction would be more appropriate. For instance, wearing a seatbelt is a legal requirement, not merely advisory; and safety benefits of wearing one are considerable indeed. To compare that to an advisory precaution which only might assist in limited

[30] [2015] EWHC 1800 (QB); [2015] 1 WLUK; [2011] EWHC 4083 (QB); [2007] EWHC 1201 (QB) respectively.

circumstances could be considered disproportionate. It remains to be seen if what sort of level will become the convention.

Finally, despite some observations in the judgment regarding the increased protective benefits of more modern models of cycle helmet[31], Griffith Williams J made no explicit comment on whether there was a reasonable obligation on the 'ordinary prudent cyclist' to purchase and wear the most up-to-date version(s). He appears to suggest that this might be an arguable issue in paragraphs 54 and 55 of his judgment, but it is submitted that any such arguments are likely to be fraught with difficulty[32]. For instance, unlike seatbelts in cars – which are fixed – the range in choice and price of cycle helmets is considerable, some affording more protection than others. Many, if not most, helmets have a scalloped design at the back which leaves a rider's occipital bone completely unprotected. From a standpoint of safety only, it is probably more prudent to wear a helmet with a fuller head covering. However, for myriad reasons, it is doubtful that in 2022 it can be realistically argued that wearing a modern helmet with a scalloped design should be considered more morally blameworthy than opting for a more protective option; after all, professional cyclists use them and if they are sold in reputable shops, a reasonable cyclist should be able to reasonably assume the helmet conforms to modern safety standards. BMX helmets tend to be more akin to a motorcycle crash helmet than standard road-bike helmets. No doubt these provide significantly greater protection, not least to the wearer's face and mouth, but again, in 2022, there has been no suggestion in a court that there is an obligation on a rider to use this type of head gear.

---

31 In particular paragraphs 50 to 52 and 54 to 55.

32 In fairness to the learned judge, his observations were prompted by the factual matrix with which he was presented: Mr Smith actually owned a helmet (though not wearing it at the time), but it was 20 years old and was considered "virtually useless" given its age and worn-out chin strap.

Similarly, there have been no pleaded cases suggesting that an old but undamaged helmet should have been updated because it no longer complied with more stringent regulations. No doubt this is because it cannot surely be a reasonable obligation upon a cyclist to update their helmet on the off chance they are involved in such a specific accident that (i) the more modern helmet will afford protection; and (ii) the more modern helmet will afford materially more protection than the old one.

One issue that was not something that needed to be considered back in 2005, is the use of helmets on cycle hire schemes. These schemes have proliferated in the United Kingdom over the last 10 to 15 years and there is a lot to commend – according to a report published in the British Medical Journal in January 2014[33], the bicycle sharing system in London at that time had an overall health benefit to many riders and has contributed to a tangible reduction air pollution; both with a smaller increase in fatalities and injuries than expected. So, as a public policy, it would seem that these schemes should be encouraged; or at least not discouraged. However, if their main selling point is convenience, is it reasonable to reduce the damages of a road traffic victim because they hopped on a bike without a helmet, when no helmet was provided? If so, is it reasonable to reduce the damages by the same amount as a road traffic victim who intended to cycle, owned a helmet, and deliberately opted not to wear it? These seem difficult propositions to justify, particularly if these schemes are to be encouraged. In Australia, it is widely accepted that the failure of both the Melbourne and Brisbane cycle hire schemes was directly due to the mandatory obligation to wear helmets. The lack of convenience was fatal.

As discussed, the lack of much case law is telling. However, it would be remiss not to deal with the few cases that have been reported. In

[33] https://www.bmj.com/content/348/bmj.g425

Reynolds v. Strutt & Parker[34], Mr Reynolds was participating in a work event, racing against other employees. He was not wearing a helmet, although at least one other competitor was. It was found by HHJ Oliver-Jones QC sitting as a High Court Judge, that the accident occurred as a result of Mr Reynolds' *"deliberate and tragically successful attempt… to force [another competitor] out of the race altogether, or, at the very least, as a result of a reckless disregard for his own safety and that of [the other competitor]."* (paragraph 26 of the judgment). In addition to the injuries sustained by his competitor, Mr Reynolds' actions caused him a permanently disabling brain injury.

HHJ Oliver-Jones QC dealt with factual causation as follows (at paragraph 32):

> *"Although the defendant had no expert evidence of its own, Dr Chinn, the claimant's expert in vehicle safety, including, in particular, the use of protective helmets, was required to attend to give oral evidence. Mr Pooles QC's cross- examination of him was limited to dealing with the speed at which it is likely the claimant was riding and the speed at which his head struck the ground.* ***That speed was, Dr Chinn opined, within the range where the use of cycle safety helmets is effective. Hence his conclusion that, if the claimant had been wearing a cycle helmet, it would have been very unlikely that he would have sustained the serious and permanently disabling brain injury that he did sustain.*** *Mr Pooles QC conceded in closing submissions (if it had ever truly been in contention) that, so far as the use of a safety helmet is concerned, the claimant had established that the absence of a helmet was causative of some injury and that, consequently, causation was not an issue that I needed to expand upon. Dr Chinn was able to confirm that there is no legal requirement to wear a cycle helmet whilst riding a bicycle on a road, although the Highway Code does*

34 [2011] EWHC 2263 (QB)

provide (at paragraph 59 of the 2007 edition) that cyclists "should wear a cycle helmet which conforms to current regulations, is the correct size and securely fastened". However, as Griffith Williams J observed in the case of Smith v Finch *[2009] EWHC 53 QB (a case in which Mr Chinn also appeared as an expert witness):*

> *"As it is accepted that the wearing of helmets may afford protection in some circumstances [and these are such circumstances in this case, in my judgment] it must follow that a cyclist of ordinary prudence would wear one, no matter whether on a long or a short trip or whether on quiet suburban roads or a busy main road."*

Although in that case the learned judge was not persuaded that the claimant's injuries would have been reduced or prevented by the wearing of a helmet, had he concluded otherwise he would have made a finding of contributory negligence against the claimant on the basis of the principles decided in the well-known case of Froom and Others v Butcher *[1976] 1 QB 286."*

Given the severity of the injuries, it is perhaps surprising that the unchallenged evidence was that a helmet would have made a material difference to Mr Reynolds' condition. However, that was the evidence, and with that in mind, HHJ Oliver-Jones QC concluded that Mr Reynold's employer (the Defendant) was one-third to blame for the injuries on the basis that had a proper risk assessment taken place, it would have been mandatory for all participants to wear a helmet. Paragraph 47:

> *"Therefore, the final matter I need to determine is how liability is to be apportioned. In making this assessment, it is not simply a matter of assessing the comparative blameworthiness of the parties, but of their respective responsibility for the damage, particularly bearing in mind the defendant's duty of care involved, on my*

> *findings, taking precautions against the claimant's own negligence. That needs to be weighed against the fact that the claimant's fault was causative of the injury he suffered.* ***In the final analysis, I need to assess both relative blameworthiness and causative potency of the parties' respective faults.*** *In my judgment, given my findings as to the claimant's responsibility for the collision, he must accept the greater proportion of blame. In these circumstances, in my judgment, a fair apportionment of liability is two thirds/one third in favour of the defendant. The claimant will thus recover one third of the damages to which he would otherwise have been entitled on a full liability basis."*

It is a relatively unusual case on its facts; and one, it is suggested, that is more useful in employer's liability claims generally than specifically cycling-related. For example, a court could well consider Mr Reynold's actions to be akin to an employee who has recklessly disregarded his own safety whilst working at height or using dangerous machinery. That said, it does show that the authority of *Smith v. Finch* has been entrenched as good law and the wearing of cycle helmets is considered to be an obviously prudent measure.

In *Phethean-Hubble v. Coles*[35] the court at first instance determined that the claimant's failure to wear a cycling helmet had no bearing on the subsequent, devastating injuries he sustained after he was struck by a car. This finding was not disturbed by the Court of Appeal when the case was considered again for other reasons of apportionment [36]. The case is still noteworthy, however, because it was unanimously found by the Court of Appeal that *"there was no reason to treat the [16 year old] claimant as if he were anything other than an adult..."*[37] . The Court did not indicate at what age a young cyclist would not be treated

[35] [2012] EWCA Civ 349; first instance decision [2011] EWHC 363 (QB).

[36] *See* para. 73 of the Court of Appeal's judgment.

[37] Paragraph 86.

"as if he were anything other than an adult". In terms of contributing factors other than wearing a helmet, this probably is not an issue – no doubt courts will be guided by the numerous authorities dealing with young pedestrians in road traffic collisions and look at the overall culpability. However, it remains to be seen whether the Court of Appeal missed an opportunity to fill a lacuna in the law regarding cycle helmets and those too young to be considered "anything other than an adult".

In short, whilst the principle of wearing a helmet is now well-established, many questions remain about the consequences of failing to do so, not least because they only make a material difference in relatively infrequent circumstances where tortious liability might arise. This could well change if and when impact-protection technology in helmets improve but for now, it is fair to say that the conventional deductions applied in seatbelt cases cannot be reliably translated across to cycle helmets.

MORE BOOKS BY LAW BRIEF PUBLISHING

A selection of our other titles available now:-

'A Practical Guide to Document Signing and Electronic Signatures for Conveyancers' by Lorraine Richardson
'A Practical Guide to Transgender Law' by Robin Moira White & Nicola Newbegin
'Artificial Intelligence – The Practical Legal Issues (2nd Edition)' by John Buyers
'A Practical Guide to Challenging Sham Marriage Allegations in Immigration Law' by Priya Solanki
'A Practical Guide to New Build Conveyancing' by Paul Sams & Rebecca East
'A Practical Guide to Inherited Wealth on Divorce' by Hayley Trim
'A Practical Guide to Shareholder Disputes in Family Businesses' by Ed Weeks
'A Practical Guide to the Law of Forests in Scotland' by Philip Buchan
'A Practical Guide to Health and Medical Cases in Immigration Law' by Rebecca Chapman & Miranda Butler
'A Practical Guide to Bad Character Evidence for Criminal Practitioners by Aparna Rao
'A Practical Guide to Environmental Enforcement' by Christopher Badger & Stuart Jessop
'A Practical Guide to Hoarding and Mental Health for Housing Lawyers' by Rachel Coyle
'A Practical Guide to Psychiatric Claims in Personal Injury – 2nd Edition' by Liam Ryan
'Stephens on Contractual Indemnities' by Richard Stephens
'A Practical Guide to the EU Succession Regulation' by Richard Frimston
'A Practical Guide to Solicitor and Client Costs – 2nd Edition' by Robin Dunne
'Constructive Dismissal – Practice Pointers and Principles' by Benjimin Burgher

'A Practical Guide to Religion and Belief Discrimination Claims in the Workplace' by Kashif Ali
'A Practical Guide to the Law of Medical Treatment Decisions' by Ben Troke
'Fundamental Dishonesty and QOCS in Personal Injury Proceedings: Law and Practice' by Jake Rowley
'A Practical Guide to the Law in Relation to School Exclusions' by Charlotte Hadfield & Alice de Coverley
'A Practical Guide to Divorce for the Silver Separators' by Karin Walker
'The Right to be Forgotten – The Law and Practical Issues' by Melissa Stock
'A Practical Guide to Planning Law and Rights of Way in National Parks, the Broads and AONBs' by James Maurici QC, James Neill et al
'A Practical Guide to Election Law' by Tom Tabori
'A Practical Guide to the Law in Relation to Surrogacy' by Andrew Powell
'A Practical Guide to Claims Arising from Fatal Accidents – 2nd Edition' by James Patience
'A Practical Guide to the Ownership of Employee Inventions – From Entitlement to Compensation' by James Tumbridge & Ashley Roughton
'A Practical Guide to Asbestos Claims' by Jonathan Owen & Gareth McAloon
'A Practical Guide to Stamp Duty Land Tax in England and Northern Ireland' by Suzanne O'Hara
'A Practical Guide to the Law of Farming Partnerships' by Philip Whitcomb
'Covid-19, Homeworking and the Law – The Essential Guide to Employment and GDPR Issues' by Forbes Solicitors
'Covid-19 and Criminal Law – The Essential Guide' by Ramya Nagesh
'Covid-19 and Family Law in England and Wales – The Essential Guide' by Safda Mahmood
'A Practical Guide to the Law of Unlawful Eviction and Harassment – 2nd Edition' by Stephanie Lovegrove
'Covid-19, Brexit and the Law of Commercial Leases – The Essential Guide' by Mark Shelton
'A Practical Guide to Costs in Personal Injury Claims – 2nd Edition' by Matthew Hoe

'A Practical Guide to the General Data Protection Regulation (GDPR) – 2nd Edition' by Keith Markham
'Ellis on Credit Hire – Sixth Edition' by Aidan Ellis & Tim Kevan
'A Practical Guide to Working with Litigants in Person and McKenzie Friends in Family Cases' by Stuart Barlow
'Protecting Unregistered Brands: A Practical Guide to the Law of Passing Off' by Lorna Brazell
'A Practical Guide to Secondary Liability and Joint Enterprise Post-Jogee' by Joanne Cecil & James Mehigan
'A Practical Guide to the Pre-Action RTA Claims Protocol for Personal Injury Lawyers' by Antonia Ford
'A Practical Guide to Neighbour Disputes and the Law' by Alexander Walsh
'A Practical Guide to Forfeiture of Leases' by Mark Shelton
'A Practical Guide to Coercive Control for Legal Practitioners and Victims' by Rachel Horman
'A Practical Guide to Rights Over Airspace and Subsoil' by Daniel Gatty
'Tackling Disclosure in the Criminal Courts – A Practitioner's Guide' by Narita Bahra QC & Don Ramble
'A Practical Guide to the Law of Driverless Cars – Second Edition' by Alex Glassbrook, Emma Northey & Scarlett Milligan
'A Practical Guide to TOLATA Claims' by Greg Williams
'A Practical Guide to Elderly Law – 2nd Edition' by Justin Patten
'A Practical Guide to the Law of Prescription in Scotland' by Andrew Foyle
'A Practical Guide to the Construction and Rectification of Wills and Trust Instruments' by Edward Hewitt
'A Practical Guide to the Law of Bullying and Harassment in the Workplace' by Philip Hyland
'How to Be a Freelance Solicitor: A Practical Guide to the SRA-Regulated Freelance Solicitor Model' by Paul Bennett
'A Practical Guide to Prison Injury Claims' by Malcolm Johnson
'A Practical Guide to the Small Claims Track - 2nd Edition' by Dominic Bright
'A Practical Guide to Advising Clients at the Police Station' by Colin Stephen McKeown-Beaumont

'A Practical Guide to Antisocial Behaviour Injunctions' by Iain Wightwick
'Practical Mediation: A Guide for Mediators, Advocates, Advisers, Lawyers, and Students in Civil, Commercial, Business, Property, Workplace, and Employment Cases' by Jonathan Dingle with John Sephton
'The Mini-Pupillage Workbook' by David Boyle
'A Practical Guide to Crofting Law' by Brian Inkster
'A Practical Guide to Spousal Maintenance' by Liz Cowell
'A Practical Guide to the Law of Domain Names and Cybersquatting' by Andrew Clemson
'A Practical Guide to the Law of Gender Pay Gap Reporting' by Harini Iyengar
'A Practical Guide to the Rights of Grandparents in Children Proceedings' by Stuart Barlow
'NHS Whistleblowing and the Law' by Joseph England
'Employment Law and the Gig Economy' by Nigel Mackay & Annie Powell
'A Practical Guide to Noise Induced Hearing Loss (NIHL) Claims' by Andrew Mckie, Ian Skeate, Gareth McAloon
'An Introduction to Beauty Negligence Claims – A Practical Guide for the Personal Injury Practitioner' by Greg Almond
'Intercompany Agreements for Transfer Pricing Compliance' by Paul Sutton
'Zen and the Art of Mediation' by Martin Plowman
'A Practical Guide to the SRA Principles, Individual and Law Firm Codes of Conduct 2019 – What Every Law Firm Needs to Know' by Paul Bennett
'A Practical Guide to Adoption for Family Lawyers' by Graham Pegg
'A Practical Guide to Industrial Disease Claims' by Andrew Mckie & Ian Skeate
'A Practical Guide to Redundancy' by Philip Hyland
'A Practical Guide to Vicarious Liability' by Mariel Irvine
'A Practical Guide to Applications for Landlord's Consent and Variation of Leases' by Mark Shelton
'A Practical Guide to Relief from Sanctions Post-Mitchell and Denton' by Peter Causton
'A Practical Guide to Equity Release for Advisors' by Paul Sams
'A Practical Guide to Financial Services Claims' by Chris Hegarty

www.ingramcontent.com/pod-product-compliance
Ingram Content Group UK Ltd.
Pitfield, Milton Keynes, MK11 3LW, UK
UKHW020151290926
15471UKWH00004B/811

9 781914 608049